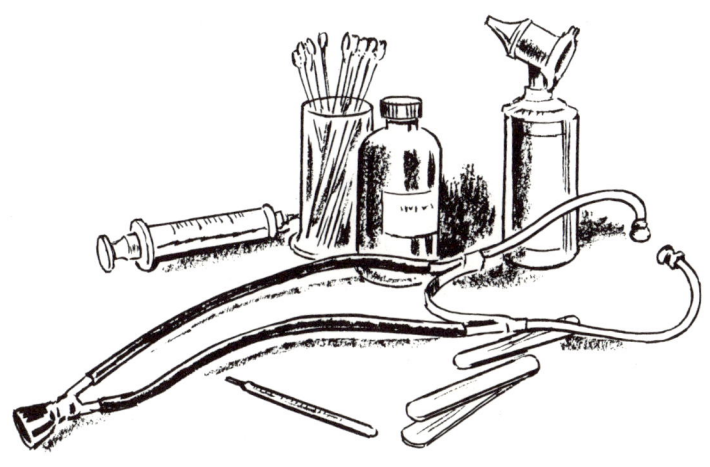

Let's Go to a Hospital

You are admitted to the hospital to have your tonsils removed. The nurse shows you your room and prepares you for the operation. While you are recovering, you meet many of the other people who make the hospital run smoothly.

Let's Go to
A Hospital

by FLORENCE WIGHTMAN ROWLAND

illustrated by Charles Dougherty

G. P. PUTNAM'S SONS   NEW YORK

The author and the artist wish to thank Mary King, R.N., Pediatrics of Morton F. Plant Hospital, Clearwater, Florida, for her help in the preparation of this book.

Text © 1968 by Florence Wightman Rowland
Library of Congress Catalog Card Number: 68-13278
PRINTED IN THE UNITED STATES OF AMERICA
Published simultaneously in the Dominion of Canada
by Longmans Canada Limited, Toronto
07211

Second Impression

For three days you have been in bed with another bad cold. But now you are feeling better. This afternoon your mother takes you to your family doctor for a checkup. She and your father have been worried about your having so many colds and sore throats this past year.

While he is checking you over, Dr. Silver uses a stethoscope on your chest. After he tells you to take some deep breaths, he listens to the sounds in your chest. When he hears the *lub-dud, lud-dud* of your heart, he says everything is all right there.

Next, Dr. Silver uses an otoscope, a special kind of flashlight with a magnifying glass and tubes that fit into your ear. The magnifying glass makes everything look much bigger than it is. With this instrument, your doctor can look down your ear canal, clear to your eardrum. If there is any inflammation or trouble, he can see it.

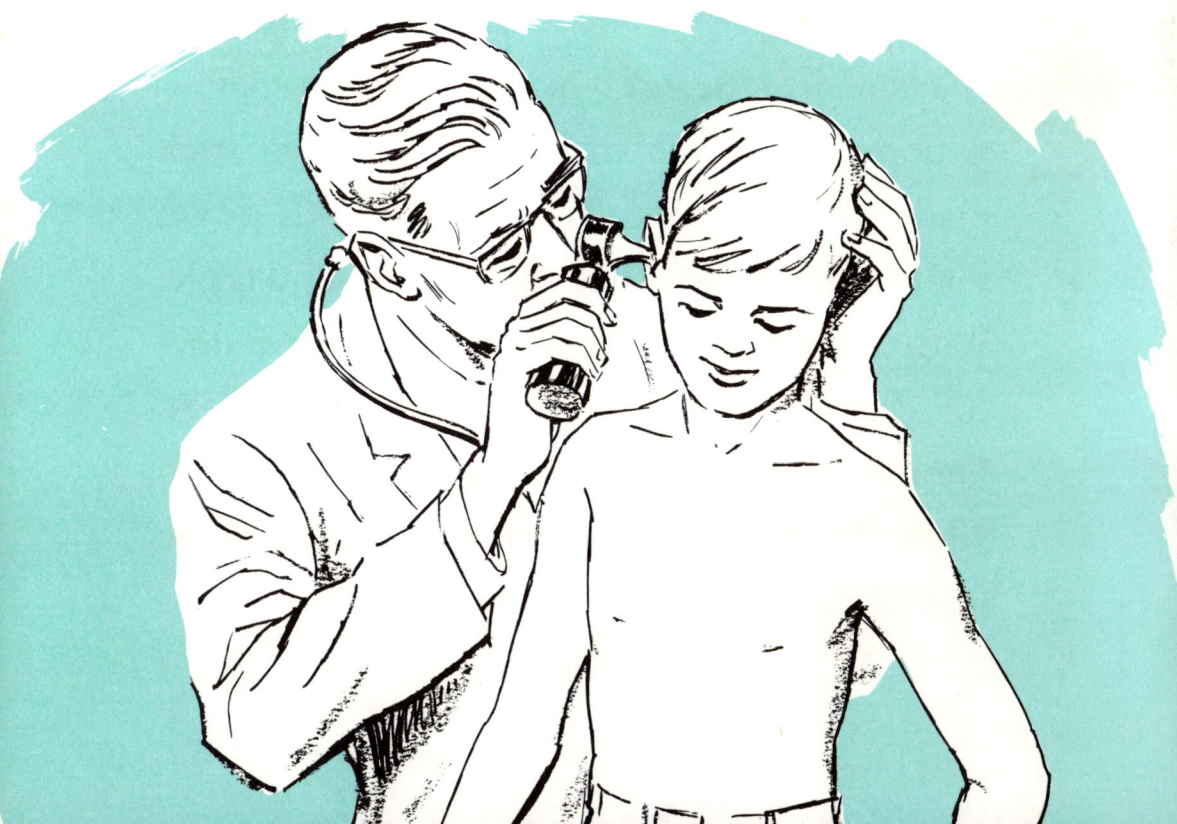

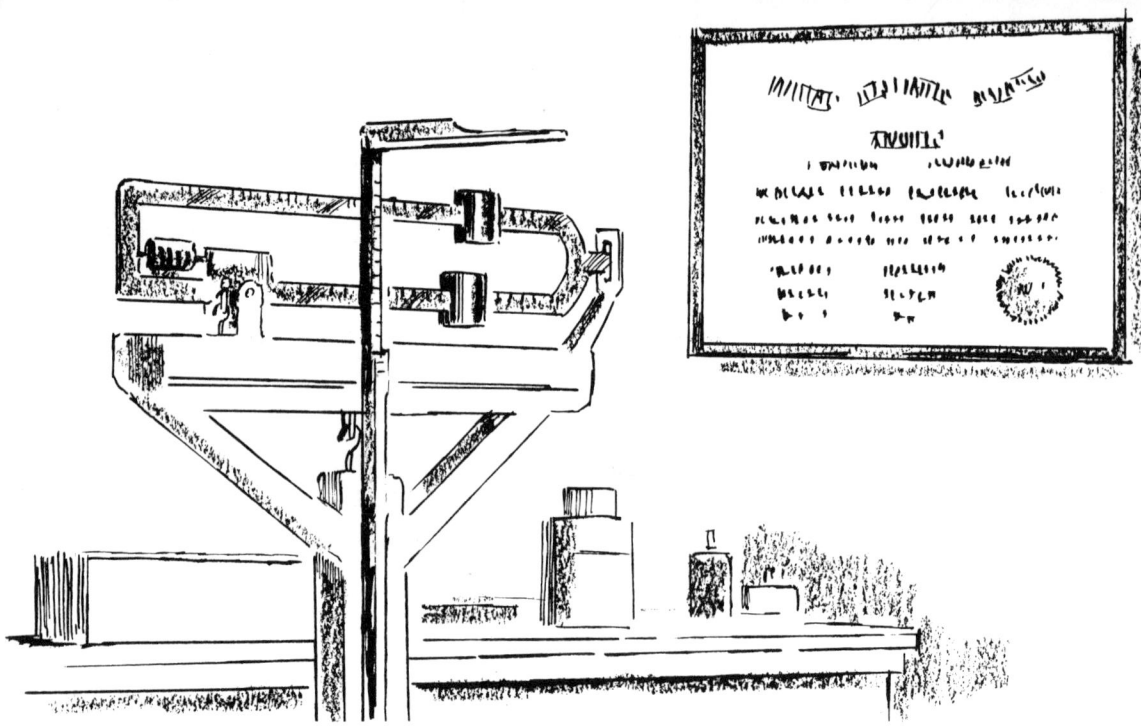

Then, just before the end of this examination, Dr. Silver picks up a tongue stick made of birchwood. With it, he holds down your tongue so that it will not wiggle. With your tongue flattened down, the doctor can see all the way down your throat. He uses a flashlight to light up your mouth while he examines it. He frowns when he sees your throat.

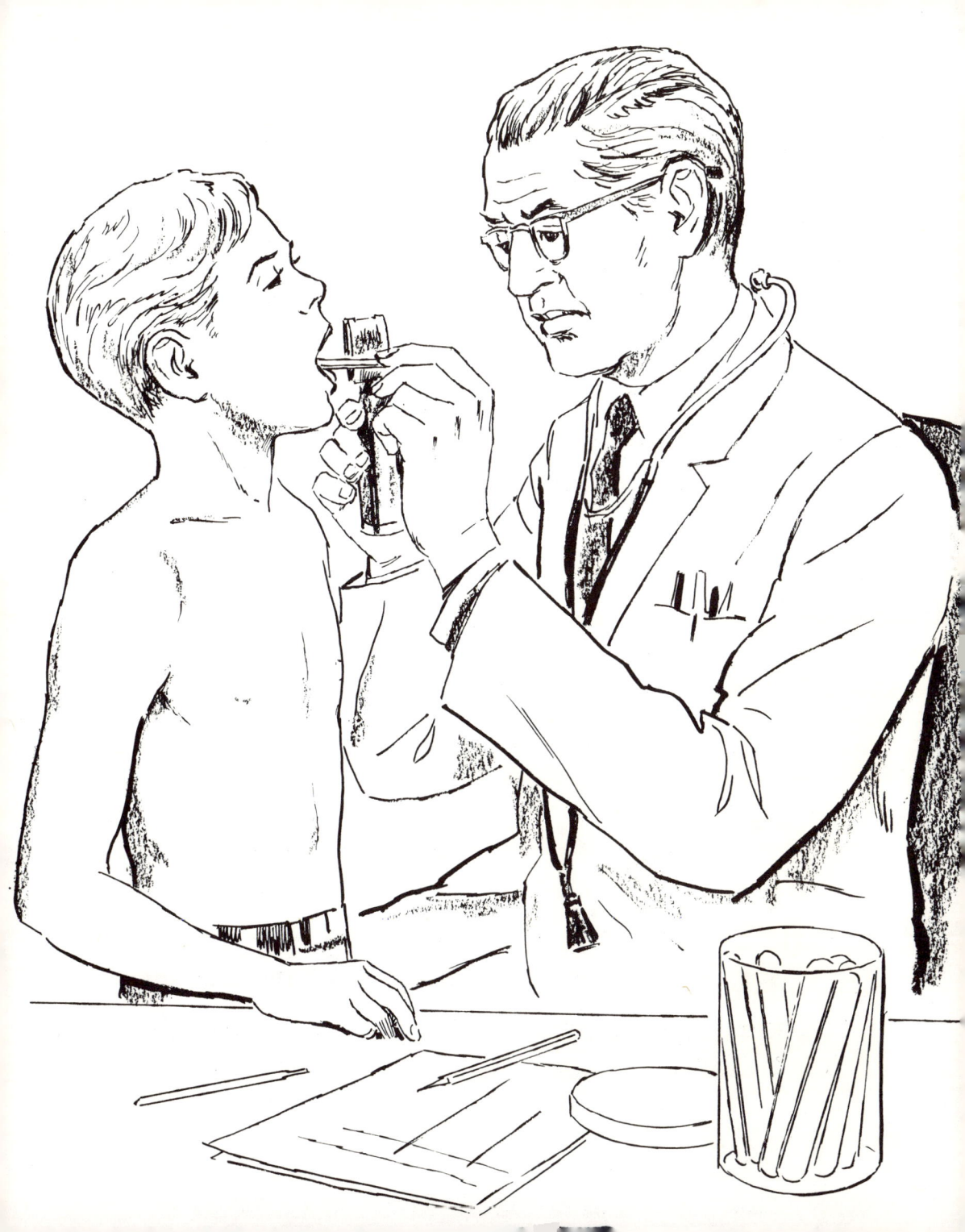

Dr. Silver now speaks to your mother about an operation to remove your tonsils.

He says it must not be put off any longer. You have to have a tonsillectomy right away. In fact, he wants you to go into the hospital that very evening after an early supper.

When the office nurse calls Grant Hospital, she finds out they have room for you in the Children's Wing on the third floor. In just a few minutes, she has made all the arrangements for you to be admitted.

No one likes to go to a hospital, even if hospitals do help make sick people well. The doctor has already told you that your throat will hurt for a few days after this operation, but after that, it will heal up. You have been in a hospital only once before, when you were born, but of course you do not remember that at all.

You tell your mother that, in a way, you look forward to having your tonsils taken out. The doctor said it could mean fewer colds for you. Then you wouldn't have to miss so much school.

Back home, mother fixes supper for you. After you have eaten, you go to your room to pack a small suitcase. You do not need much. After all, you will probably be in the hospital only two nights.

Into your suitcase, you put a pair of clean pajamas, your bedroom slippers, a comb and a brush, your toothbrush and toothpaste and your bathrobe. Before snapping the lid shut, you remember to take along the book you have been reading. Maybe you will get time to finish it while you are there.

As soon as you are ready to leave, you say good-bye to your father, who has to stay home with your little brother. Then you and your mother climb into the car, and she drives you to the hospital. After finding a space in the parking lot in front of the five-story building, you walk toward the front door.

As you step on the rubber mat, the big doors fly open, just like the ones in the grocery store. In you go. When you walk past the big lounge on your right, you see many people waiting for Visiting Hour to begin. A few hold bunches of flowers. Others carry gifts wrapped in gay paper and tied with ribbons.

At the Information Desk, your mother finds out you have to go down the hall four doors to the Admission Office. You wait there until the clerk brings your entrance papers. She asks you your name, your age, where you live, and your phone number. When she wants to know who your nearest relative is, you shrug your shoulders, not knowing what she means. Your mother smiles and tells the young woman her name. Then she shows her your family's hospitalization card that will help to pay for your stay here.

The admission clerk tells your mother your doctor has ordered a blood count, a chest X-ray, and a urinalysis. First you are to go to the laboratory farther down the hall, then return to the Admission Office.

You and your mother walk down the hall to the laboratory. The nurse in the office there has a big smile for you as you enter the small room.

She explains that first she will get a drop of blood from your finger. Holding the forefinger of your right hand tightly,

she pricks the tip with a finger stick needle. Because she knows just how to do this, it hurts only a second.

As soon as a big drop of blood appears at the end of your finger, she spreads it on a glass slide. This slide will then be studied by a laboratory technician at one of the many microscopes inside the workroom.

After making the blood slide ready to send into the laboratory, the nurse hands you a small urine specimen bottle. She tells you to go into the office bathroom and fill it, so that tests can be made of your urine to find out if you are in good health.

In the next room, another technician takes a chest X-ray to make sure your lungs are in good condition.

As soon as this is done, you and your mother go back to the Admission Office. There a clerk is waiting to take you to your room.

Carrying your suitcase, she leads the way to the elevator and up you go. On the third floor, you follow the clerk through a big swinging door. She holds it open for you. And there you are, in the Children's Wing.

On your left, you pass a small lounge where visitors may rest and talk. To your right, you see a glassed-in room, the nurses' station. Here the patients' records are kept. Many medicines and supplies are also in the nurses' station.

Out of this shiny place comes a white-uniformed nurse with a pretty cap perched on top of her dark hair. Miss Carter smiles at you, a nice, friendly smile. You like her at once.

Miss Carter tells you to come along with her to get weighed and measured in the Treatment Room. When you enter the Treatment Room, you see bottles and boxes of supplies stacked on shelves along one wall. In the center is a table and two chairs, and in one corner stands the big scale where you will be weighed.

You step up on it and watch the balance arm with its movable marker that swings to the right. After Miss Carter records your weight, she finds out how tall you are with the scale's sliding, vertical ruler that measures your height.

Now you go to your room. As soon as you sit down, Miss Carter pops a thermometer in your mouth under your tongue to find out if your body is the right temperature and not too hot.

While you hold the thermometer in your mouth, you look around. This ward has four beds, two on each side, and there is a spotless bathroom near the door. Since you are the only patient in it so far, you hope others will come soon to keep you company.

After removing the thermometer from your mouth, Miss Carter brings in your name band and puts it around your right wrist. While she chats with your mother, you stare at the gay yellow drapes at the long windows. Dancing clowns are printed all over them. Then you look up. There high above your head, hanging from the ceiling, are two television sets.

This is a nice surprise. You did not expect to enjoy television here. But this is a modern hospital, and the Children's Wing is new. It has been open only a few weeks.

Now Miss Carter is showing you how to work the intercom buttons. On your bed lie the controls. "Look," says Miss Carter, "all you have to do when you want to talk to a nurse is to press the button marked N. That rings a bell in the nurses' station. A nurse on duty there picks up a receiver and asks you what you need. Whatever it is, she sees that it is taken care of right away."

Miss Carter explains that, at the same time, a light flashes on outside the door of this ward. If a nurse happens to be going by, she comes in to find out what you want.

Now you examine the other controls. By pressing the television button, you turn on one of the sets. Then you flip the dial around until the right program comes on. Now, while you are watching, you see the pictures flash by, one by one. It will be fun to tune in your favorite programs while you lie in bed.

Many hospitals do not yet have these intercoms or television in every room. However, they do have a signal button pinned to each bed. When you turn it on, a light shows outside the door to alert the nurses that you need something.

Hospitals are very much like small towns. Instead of a Mayor, there is an Administrator. He hires the staff and keeps everything going along smoothly.

Besides nurses and doctors and laboratory technicians, there are other important people who make you comfortable and help you get well. Some keep the halls and rooms neat and clean. Others cook the meals that you enjoy. Many run huge dishwashers and do the laundry so that you can have fresh sheets and towels and blankets.

There are many who work at other tasks. You saw a few of these when you arrived. The lady at the Information Desk. The clerk in the Admission Office who took you up to your room. As you passed the gift shop and coffee bar, you saw other workers waiting on customers. It takes many people to staff a well-run hospital.

Long ago, when there were no hospitals to go to, you stayed home and your family doctor had to come to see you. Also, there

were no registered nurses then. A friend, a neighbor or a member of your family did what they could to make you comfortable.

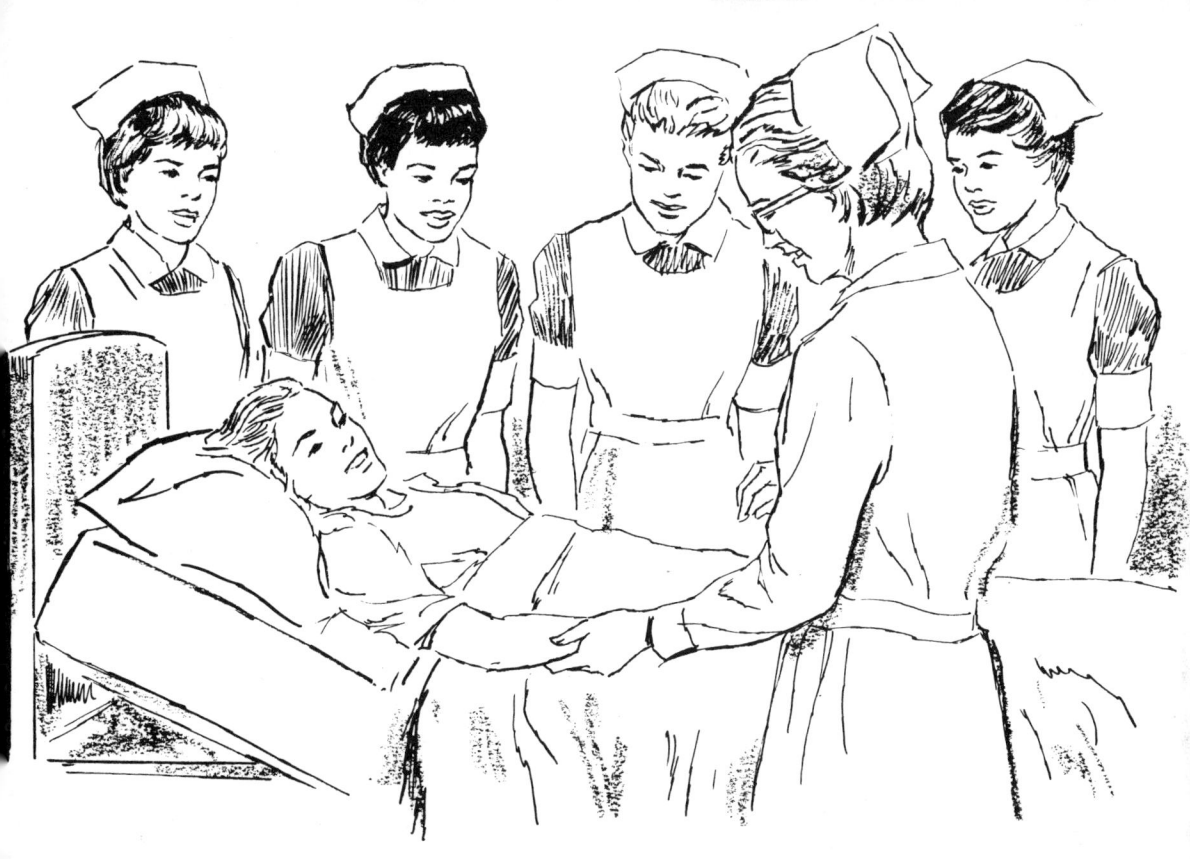

Today young women go to special schools to study how to be nurses. They work in hospitals to learn how to help patients to get well. When they finish all the courses, they graduate, but not until they pass the state examinations do they become registered nurses.

The end of Visiting Hour is close now. Before your mother goes home, she helps you get into your pajamas and tucks you in bed. Then she hangs your clothes in the closet.

Saying she will be back in the morning before your operation, your mother kisses you good-bye. She stops near the door to look back at you and smile. Then she tells you to be good and to mind the nurses.

Only a few minutes later, just as you snap on the television set on your side of the room, a nurse walks in. She helps you wash up and get ready to go to sleep.

When you wake up in the morning, the first person you see is your mother. She is sitting in a chair next to your bed. After you talk a while, a nurse comes to take your temperature and wash you up.

After she leaves, a tall young man walks briskly into the room. He is an intern. Since Grant Hospital is connected with the medical school nearby, their new young doctors get part of their training examining hospital patients and learning from older doctors.

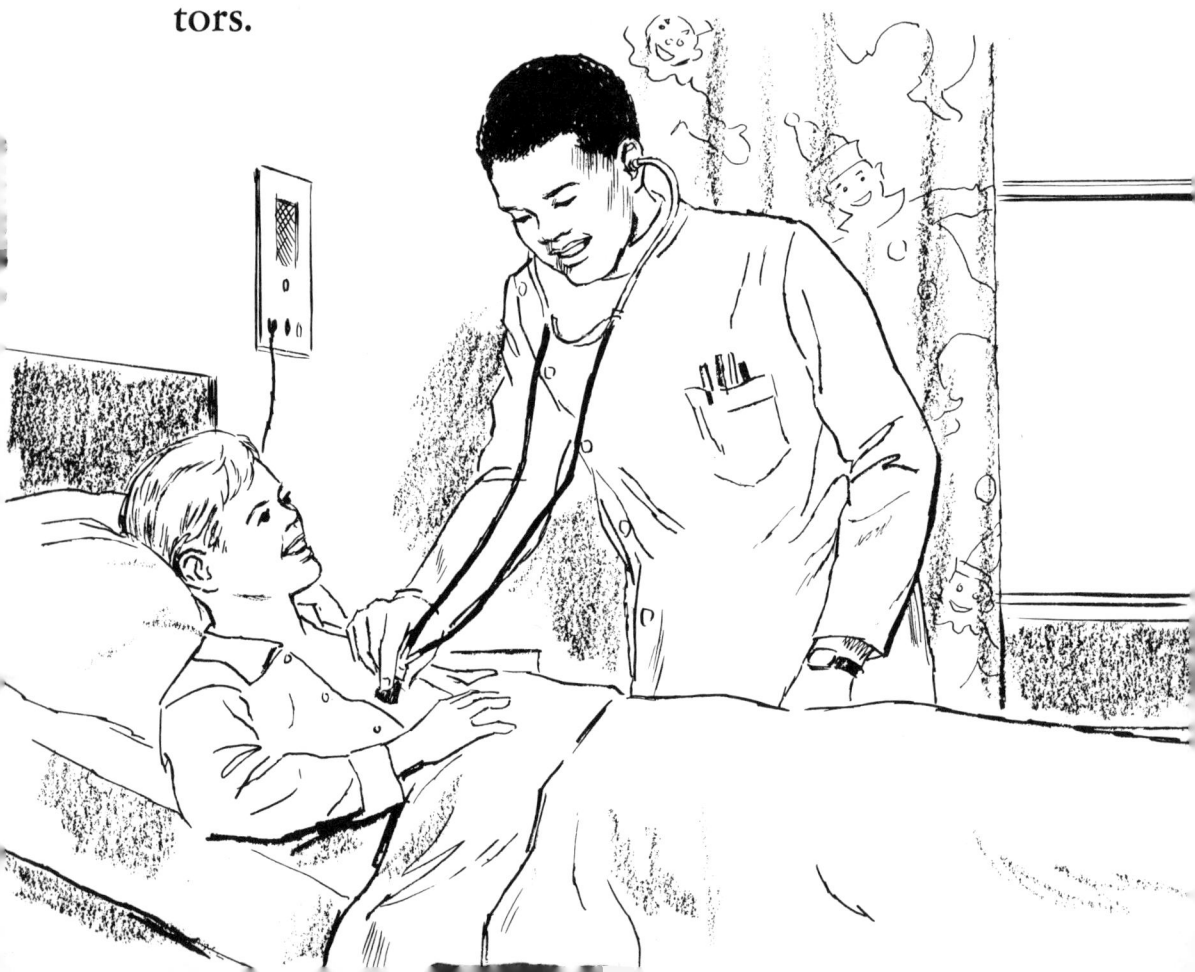

Just as your family doctor did, this doctor uses a tongue stick to hold your tongue down, so he can look at your tonsils. He listens to the sounds in your chest with his stethoscope and examines your ears, too.

Such examinations help the intern to learn the skills he will need to know in order to help those who are ill or hurt. After he is finished with his training, he will set up an office somewhere and care for his own patients.

When the intern leaves, a nurse comes to help you change into hospital pajamas and to get you ready for the operation. After she ties the baggy garment together in the back, you look back over your shoulder at the droopy seat. You are sure you look as funny as a comical clown in a circus. When you see your mother trying to hide a smile, you have to laugh, and the nurse does too.

Soon another nurse comes to give you an injection. She tells you to climb into bed and lie on your stomach. You hardly feel the prick of the needle.

Before she leaves, this nurse explains that the injection will help you fall asleep by the time you go up to the Operating Room less than an hour from now. Then she tells you that you will be taken to the Operating Room in your bed and returned to this ward still in your bed.

And that is just what happens. Before long, your eyelids feel heavy. They shut, and you do not feel like opening them. Soon your mother's voice sounds farther and farther away. You hardly feel your bed being rolled toward the door.

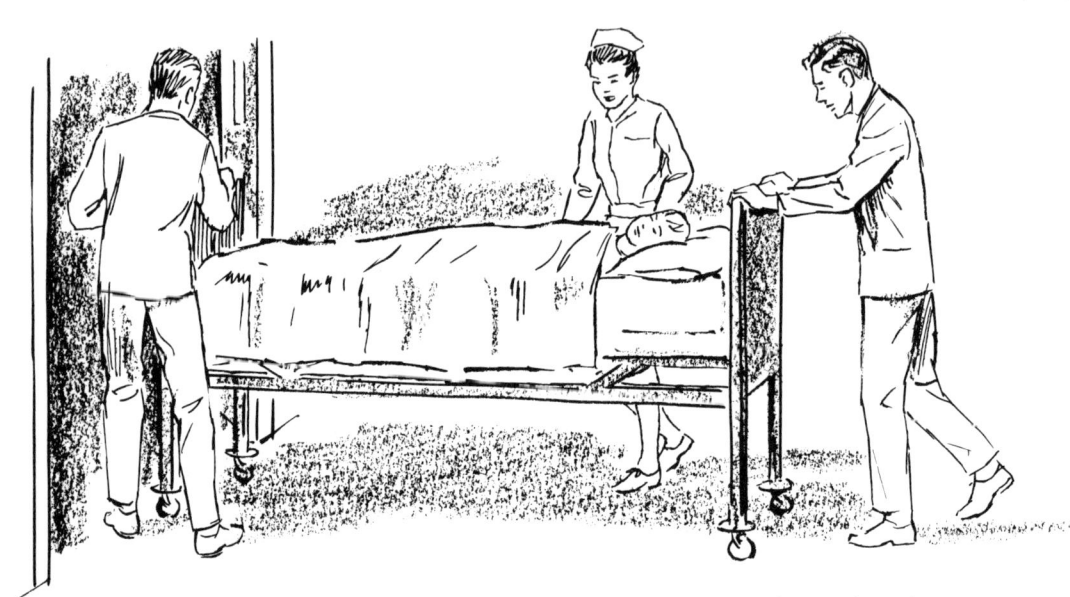

When you open your eyes again, it is hours later. You are back in your ward, and all you want to do is sleep, sleep, sleep.

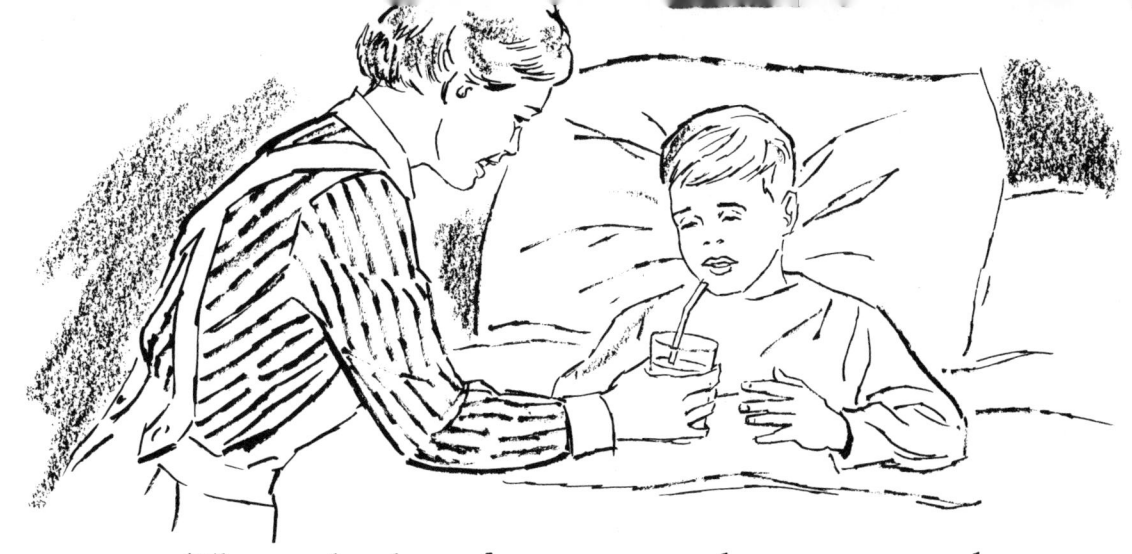

Through that day, you wake up several times, but mostly you sleep. During the afternoon, a pretty young girl comes in. She is a nurse's aid, wearing a blue striped uniform with a white apron. She brings you sparkling ginger ale to sip, and you are grateful. It helps to cool your hot mouth.

Each time you look, you see your mother, sitting nearby. Once you reach far out to touch her cheek. It is such a comfort to have her there even though you do not feel like talking.

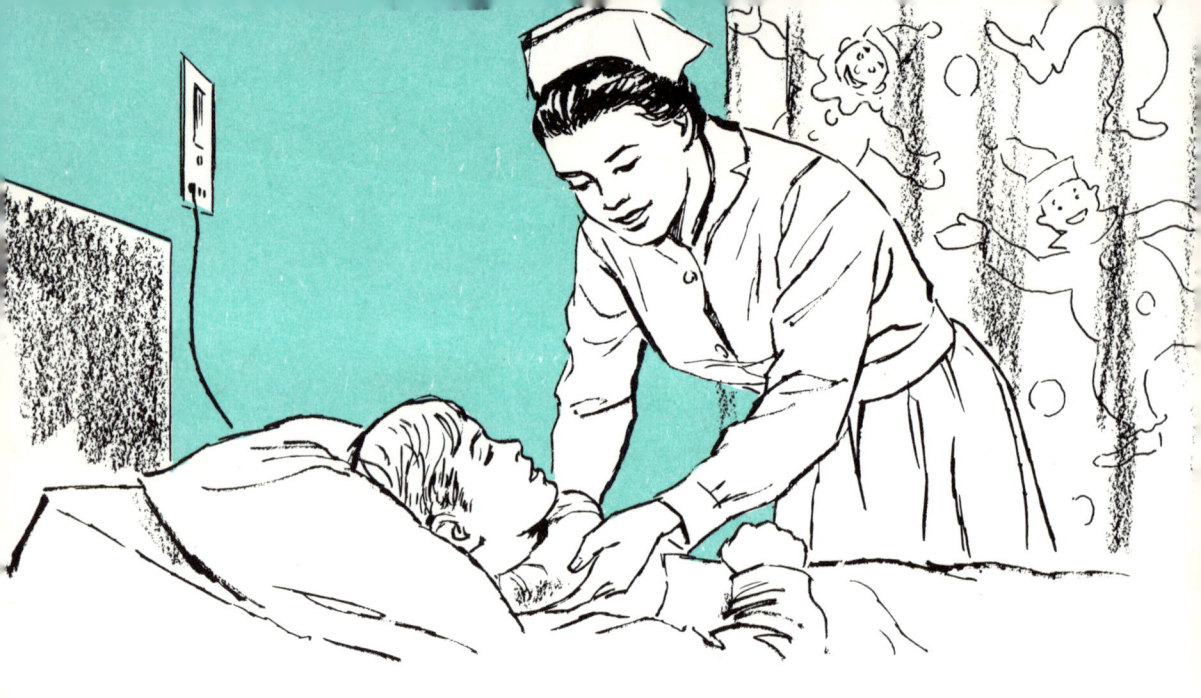

In the middle of the afternoon, your throat still hurts. Picking up the intercom controls, you push the N button. You tell the nurse who answers that your throat is sore. It is hard for you to speak to her. She says she will bring you something to make you feel better.

Before long, she comes in with a plastic ice collar to put around your neck and covers it with a towel. It looks like a life preserver, only smaller, and it takes away most of the hurt. In fact, you are soon so much better that you ask for a dish of chocolate ice cream. At suppertime, the same pretty nurse's aid brings a tray to you. On it is more ice cream and a dish of red jello.

Once more your mother stays with you until the end of Visiting Hour that evening. She tells you she will be back in the morning after breakfast. Then, if your doctor lets you leave the hospital, she will drive you home. There you will spend a few more days in bed before you are ready to go back to school.

At ten o'clock in the morning, you are dressed in your own clothes, sitting in a wheelchair, ready to leave. You say goodbye to the friendly nurses who took such good care of you. Then away you go. Your stay at the hospital is over.

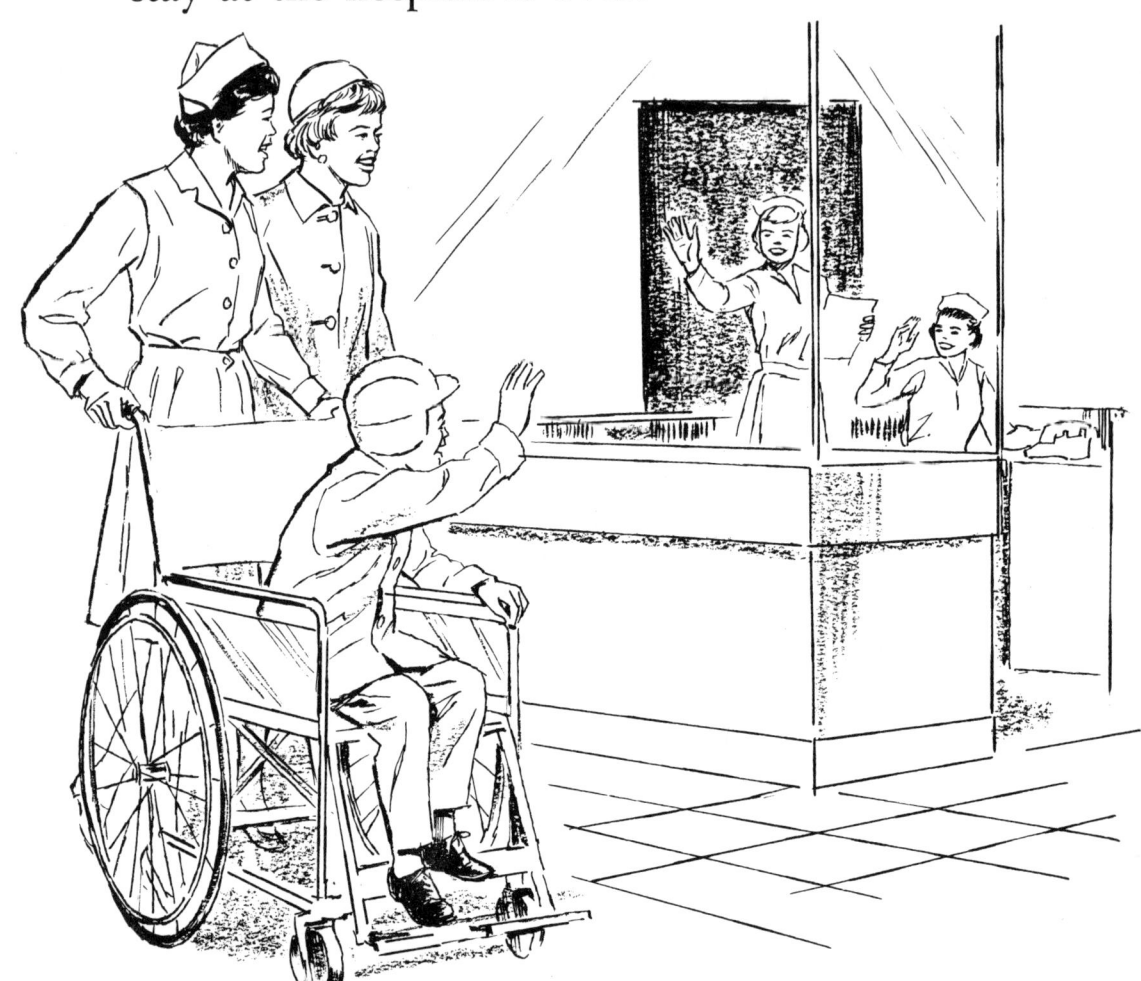

Other Things to Do While Reading
Let's Go to a Hospital

1. Look at the yellow pages of your telephone book to find the names and locations of the hospitals in your town. Which hospital is nearest to your home?
2. If your family carries hospitalization insurance, ask to read the contract to see what is covered by this insurance.
3. Draw a picture of the cap worn by a registered nurse in one of the hospitals in your town.
4. Pretend you are a reporter. Interview someone in your family about his stay in the hospital. Why did he go? How long did he stay? What kinds of tests did he have?
5. Make a list of questions that you think the Admission Office of a hospital needs to ask its patients.
6. With a classmate, act out the visit to the doctor when he decides you need a tonsillectomy.
7. Make a list of the things you would take to a hospital if you knew you were going to stay a week.
8. You are to take medicine every three hours from seven o'clock in the morning until 7 o'clock at night. At what time do you take the other doses?
9. Listen to some records and find some soothing music that you would like to hear if you were a patient in the hospital.

Other Books about Hospitals

Pyne, Mable, *The Hospital* (Boston, Houghton Mifflin Company, 1962).
Coy, Harold, *The First Book of Hospitals* (New York, Franklin Watts).

Glossary

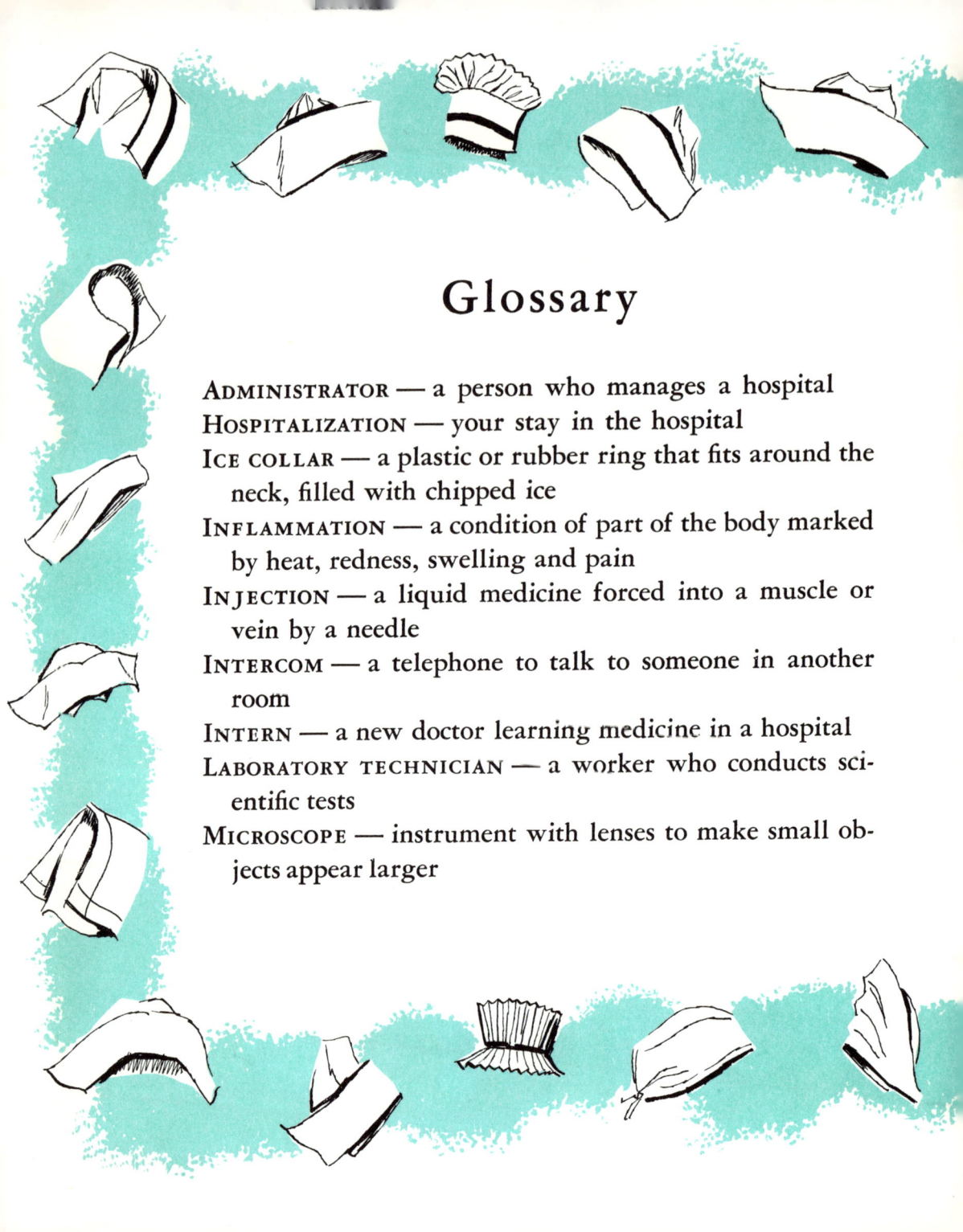

Administrator — a person who manages a hospital

Hospitalization — your stay in the hospital

Ice collar — a plastic or rubber ring that fits around the neck, filled with chipped ice

Inflammation — a condition of part of the body marked by heat, redness, swelling and pain

Injection — a liquid medicine forced into a muscle or vein by a needle

Intercom — a telephone to talk to someone in another room

Intern — a new doctor learning medicine in a hospital

Laboratory technician — a worker who conducts scientific tests

Microscope — instrument with lenses to make small objects appear larger

Nurse's aid — a person who helps the nurse

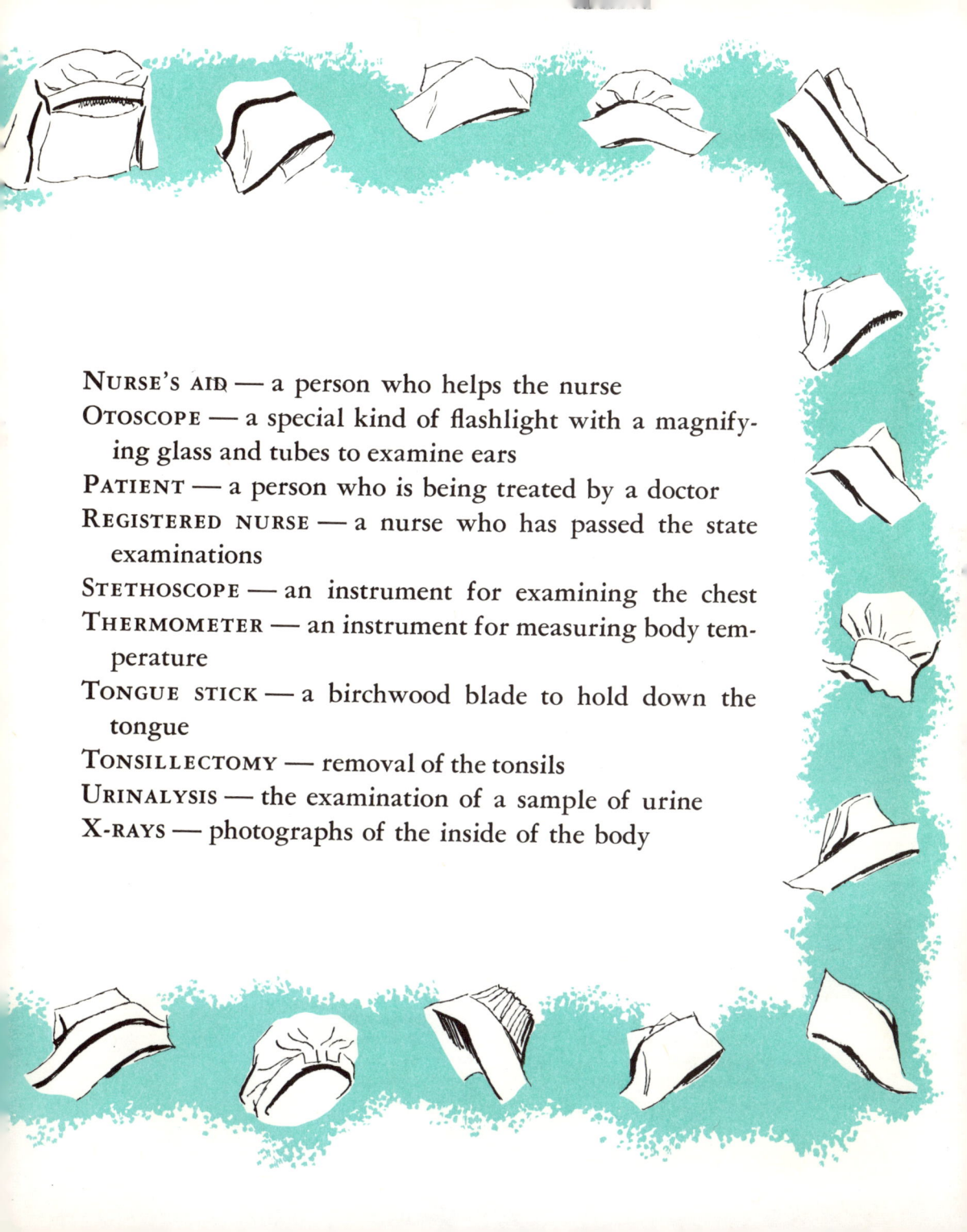

Otoscope — a special kind of flashlight with a magnifying glass and tubes to examine ears

Patient — a person who is being treated by a doctor

Registered nurse — a nurse who has passed the state examinations

Stethoscope — an instrument for examining the chest

Thermometer — an instrument for measuring body temperature

Tongue stick — a birchwood blade to hold down the tongue

Tonsillectomy — removal of the tonsils

Urinalysis — the examination of a sample of urine

X-rays — photographs of the inside of the body

OTHER TITLES IN THE POPULAR *LET'S GO* SERIES

Science
- to an Atomic Energy Town
- for a Nature Walk
- to a Planetarium
- to a Rocket Base
- on a Space Trip
- to a Weather Station
- to the Moon
- to a Fish Hatchery

Health
- to a Dentist
- to a Hospital

Communications
- to a Telephone Company
- to a Television Station

Food and Clothing
- to a Bakery
- to a Candy Factory
- to a Clothing Factory
- to a Dairy
- to a Farm

Commerce and Industry
- to an Automobile Factory
- to a Steel Mill

Transportation
- to an Airport
- to a Freight Yard
- to a Harbor
- to a Truck Terminal
- to Build a Suspension Bridge

Conservation
- to a Dam
- to a National Park
- to Stop Air Pollution
- to Stop Water Pollution

American History
- to Colonial Williamsburg
- to Mount Vernon
- to an Indian Cliff Dwelling

Armed Services
- to Annapolis
- to the U.S. Air Force Academy
- to West Point
- to the U.S. Coast Guard Academy
- aboard an Atomic Submarine

Government — Local
- to a City Hall
- to a Court
- to Vote

Government — National and International
- to the Capitol
- to the F.B.I.
- to the Supreme Court
- to the United Nations Headquarters
- to the U.S. Mint
- to the White House
- to See Congress at Work
- to the Peace Corps

Recreation
- to an Aquarium
- to a Circus
- to a World's Fair
- to a Zoo

Community — Commercial
- to a Bank
- to a Garage
- to a Newspaper
- to a Supermarket
- to Watch a Building Go Up

Community — Government
- to a Firehouse
- to a Library
- to a Police Station
- to a Post Office
- to a Sanitation Department
- to a School

Geography
- to Europe
- to South America
- to India